Hawai'i's
BENTO BOX
Cookbook

Fun Lunches for Kids

Susan Yuen

Mutual Publishing

Library of Congress Cataloging-in-Publication Data

Yuen, Susan.
  Hawaii's Bento box cookbook : how to make fun lunches for kids / Susan Yuen.
      p. cm.
  Includes index.
  ISBN-13: 978-1-56647-865-6 (wire-o softcover : alk. paper)
  ISBN-10: 1-56647-865-0 (wire-o softcover : alk. paper)
  1. Lunchbox cookery. 2. Bento cookery. 3. Cookery, Japanese. 4. Hawaiian cookery. I. Title.
  TX735.Y84 2008
  641.5'34--dc22

                                2008019446

ISBN-10: 1-56647-865-0
ISBN-13: 978-1-56647-865-6

Design by Courtney Young

First Printing, July 2008
Second Printing, April 2009

Mutual Publishing, LLC
1215 Center Street, Suite 210
Honolulu, Hawai'i 96816
Ph: (808) 732-1709 / Fax: (808) 734-4094
email: info@mutualpublishing.com
www.mutualpublishing.com

Printed in Korea

Hawai'i's
BENTO BOX
Cookbook

Table of Contents

Part II—'Ono Recipes

Acknowledgments

I wish to thank God first and foremost for giving me the gift of life in so many different ways and for giving me the opportunity to write this book. May this book serve to glorify You.

I also want to thank Mark, Paige, and Sean Patric, for the love, help, patience, and great support that they give me day in and day out. Mark, or should I say, "Tacky," you are the love of my life and best friend; life would be extremely boring without you! Words cannot express all of the joy, excitement, and laughter that you bring to my life.

To my mom, Geraldine, thank you so much for taking so much of your time to babysit so that I could complete this book. Thank you Mom also for teaching me how to cook and how to enjoy feeding others! I love you!

To Mom and Dad Yuen, thank you for your love, encouragement, excitement, and advice.

To my other family members and friends, thank you so much for your enthusiasm, secret recipes, advice, and support. I am extremely blessed to be surrounded by such positive and loving relatives and friends.

I especially want to thank Lori-Ann for her computer skills, brilliant ideas, great friendship, and for telling me that I should submit this book to a publisher!

Thanks also to Mutual Publishing for allowing me the opportunity to write this book.

Finally, I want to thank Paige again, for she provided the impetus and inspiration for this book, and she forever changed my perspective on life from the day she was born. Paige, if you're reading this, I want you to know that this book and all the "special" meals that I have made and continue to make for you today were and are made with my greatest love for you. Hopefully, when you are older, you will open this book and see that your lunches were made with the magical spirit of "Aloha"!

PART I
BENTOS

keiki cutouts

Ballerina
with Chicken Katsu and Tamago

INGREDIENTS

1 slice bologna
1 slice cheddar cheese
5 slices kamaboko
Nori for mouth and eyes
Cake decorations (silver dragées and flower decorations)
Chicken Katsu (see page 99)
Tamago (see page 134)

1. With the bologna, use the circle cutter to cut out the girl's body. Then use the rabbit cutter to cut out the girl's head. Rotate the rabbit cutter 180 degrees to cut off the rabbit ears. Use one of the ears to make the girl's feet by cutting it in half.

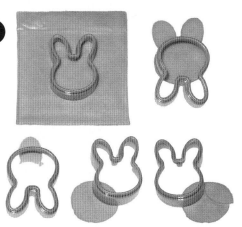

2. With the cheddar cheese, use the rabbit cutter to cut out the rabbit shape. Rotate the rabbit cutter 180 degrees to cut off the rabbit ears. Use the bottom edge of the rabbit cutter to cut out the bangs of the girl's hair. Cut off ½ of the rabbit's ear from the bottom. Use the top part of the ear for the girl's bun.

3. With the kamaboko, use the teardrop-shaped cutter to cut out 5 teardrops. Cut off 2 of the pointed top part of the teardrops about ⅓ of the way down to use as the top part of the dress. It will look like triangles.

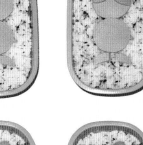

With nori, punch out mouth and eyes.

4. Place the bologna head, the body of the girl, and her feet on a flat bed of rice. Use the cheese cutouts for the girl's bangs and the small cut rabbit ear as the bun for her hair. Place the 3 teardrop-shaped kamaboko about ⅓ of the way down her body to form her skirt. Then place the 2 triangular kamaboko cutouts above the skirt to form the top of her dress. Add eyes and a mouth. Then add the silver dragées to form the trim of her dress and hairpiece, and use the blue flowers to decorate the dress.

INGREDIENTS

Rice
1 slice bologna
1 slice cheddar cheese
8 thin slices kamaboko
Red, purple, green, yellow, and blue Color Mist™
Decorative wooden pick
Nori for eyes and mouth
Somen (see page 123)
Garlicky Shrimp (see page 111)

1. Place rice in container. With the bologna, use the circle cutter to cut out the boy's body. Then use the rabbit cutter to cut out the boy's head. Rotate the rabbit cutter 180 degrees to cut off the rabbit ears and discard.

2. With the cheddar cheese, use the rabbit cutter to cut out the rabbit shape. Rotate the rabbit cutter 180 degrees to cut off the rabbit ears and discard. Use the bottom edge of the rabbit cutter to cut out the boy's hair.

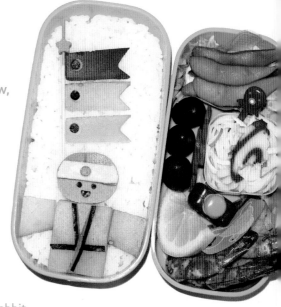

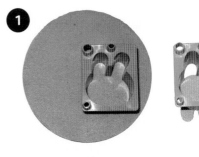

3. Take the kamaboko slices and spray 1 slice red, 1 slice purple, 1 slice green, 1 slice yellow, and 3 slices blue. Cut a fish shape out of the red, purple, and green kamaboko with a knife. Cut a headband for the boy out of the yellow kamaboko with a knife. Then using a small square cutter or a knife, cut out the boy's coat. Also cut a small blue circle for the boy's headband. Cut out 3 circles for the fish eyes out of the last white slice of kamaboko.

4. To assemble, place the bologna head and body on the rice along with the wooden pick to use as a flagstaff. Then add the boy's hair, coat, headband with the blue kamboko circle, and the fish. Add the kamaboko fish eyes and cut out small nori circles to finish the fish eyes. Cut out thin strips of nori for the boy's coat trim and belt. Cut out nori eyes and a mouth to complete the boy.

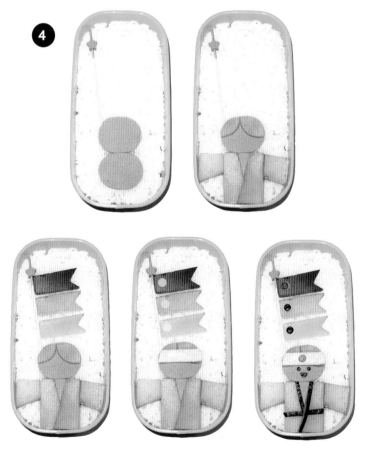

INGREDIENTS

Rice
1 slice bologna
1 slice cheddar cheese
3 slices kamaboko sprayed with pink Color Mist
Nori for eyes and mouth
Cake decorations for buttons and hair decorations
Wontons (see page 95)
Beef with Broccoli (see page 78)

1. Place rice in container. With the bologna, cut out 2 circles for the girl's head and arms, and 2 small teardrop shapes for the feet. Cut two opposite sides of one of the bologna circles to make the girl's arms.

2. With the cheese, cut a half circle and 2 small teardrop shapes for the girl's hair.

With 2 slices of the pink kamaboko, cut out the girl's dress. Also from the kamaboko, cut out a small rectanglé for the collar of the dress and two small flowers for her hair.

3. To assemble the girl, arrange her head, dress, arms, and feet on the rice. Add her hair, the kamaboko flowers, and nori eyes and mouth. Then add the cake decorations to make the flowers and buttons on her dress.

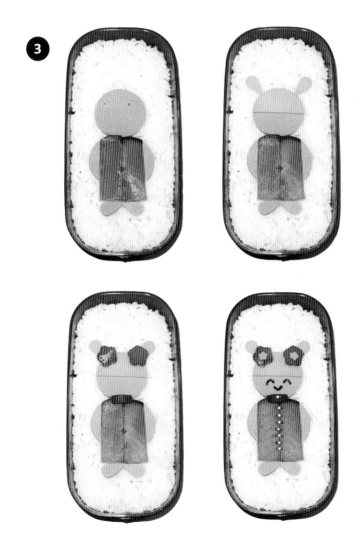

Hula Girl

with Chicken Long Rice and Kālua Pork

INGREDIENTS

1 slice bologna
1 slice cheddar cheese
5 slices kamaboko
1 teaspoon green hana ebi (Japanese colored shrimp flakes)
Nori for mouth and eyes
Cake decorations for earrings and flower
Chicken Long Rice (see page 116)
Slow Cooker Kālua Pork (see page 93)

1. With the bologna, use the circle cutter to cut out the girl's body. Then use the rabbit cutter to cut out the girl's head. Rotate the rabbit cutter 180 degrees to cut off the rabbit ears. Use one of the ears to make the girl's feet by cutting it in half.

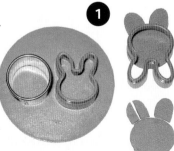

2. With the cheddar cheese, use the rabbit cutter to cut out the rabbit shape. Rotate the rabbit cutter 180 degrees to cut off the rabbit ears. Use the bottom edge of the rabbit cutter to cut out the bangs of the girl's hair. Also cut out a top for the girl using the "figure eight" shape cutter.

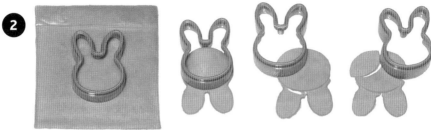

3. With the kamaboko, cut out three long teardrops to make the hula skirt. Also cut out one small flower for the girl's hair.

With nori, punch out a mouth and eyes.

4. Place the bologna head and the body of the girl on a flat bed of rice. Use the cheese cutouts for the girl's bangs and the rabbit ears as the girl's pigtails. Press the long teardrop-shaped kamaboko into the green ebi and place on the girl's body to form a skirt. Place the "figure eight" cheese top over the top of the skirt. Add bologna feet, eyes, and mouth, and the kamaboko flower for her hair. Add cake decorations to finish her flower and for her earrings.

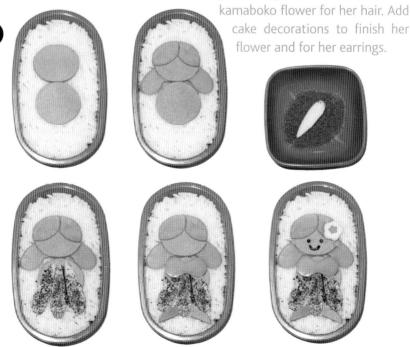

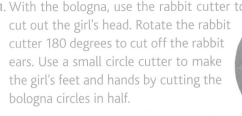

INGREDIENTS

Rice
1 slice bologna
1 slice cheddar cheese
4 slices kamaboko
Pink Color Mist
Nori for eyes
Cake decorations for hair and kimono
Shoyu Chicken Drumettes (see page 107)
Fried Udon (see page 119)

1. With the bologna, use the rabbit cutter to cut out the girl's head. Rotate the rabbit cutter 180 degrees to cut off the rabbit ears. Use a small circle cutter to make the girl's feet and hands by cutting the bologna circles in half.

2. With the cheddar cheese, use the rabbit cutter to cut out the rabbit shape. Rotate rabbit cutter 180 degrees to cut off the rabbit ears. Use the bottom edge of the rabbit cutter to cut out the bangs of the girl's hair. Cut off ½ of the rabbit's ear from the bottom. Use the top part of the ear for the girl's bun.

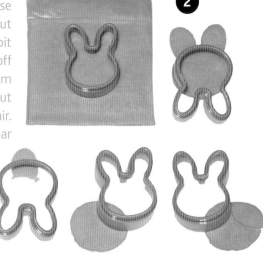

Spray 3 slices of the kamaboko with pink Color Mist. Cut out the girl's mouth, a small flower, and the sleeves of the kimono out of 1 slice of the pink kamaboko. With the last white slice of kamaboko, cut a sash for the kimono.

3. Arrange the girl's bologna head and pink kimono. Add the cheese hair, sash, and hands and feet. Place the kamaboko flower in the girl's hair and decorate her hair and the sash with the cake decorations. Add her nori eyes and kamaboko mouth.

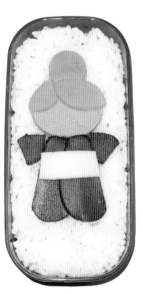

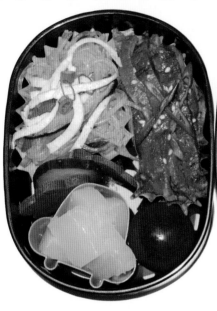

INGREDIENTS

Rice
1 slice bologna
1 slice cheddar cheese
1 cooked hotdog
Nori for eyes and mouth
Cake decorations for shorts
Chap Chae (see page 115)
Barbeque Beef (see page 77)

1. Place rice in the container. Cut out 3 circles from the bologna for the boy's **1** head, arms, and body. Cut the opposite sides of one of the circles to make arms. Cut out a circle to make the boy's hair (see picture) and cut out his shorts from the cheese. Slice the hotdog on the bias to make a surfboard.

2. To assemble the boy, arrange the bologna head, body, arms, and feet. Add the boy's cheese hair and shorts, and his hotdog surfboard. Then cut his eyes and mouth out of the nori and place on his face. Add cake decorations to his shorts to complete.

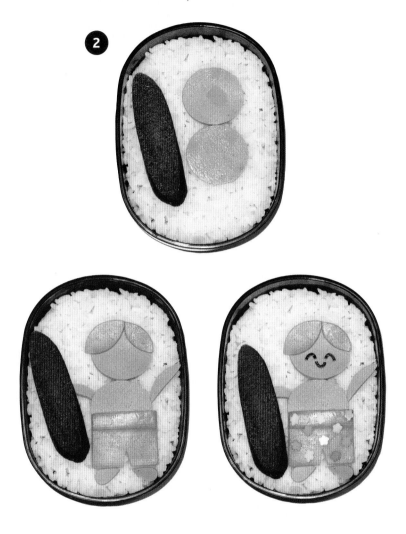

INGREDIENTS

1 hotdog
2 Teriyaki Meatballs (recipe follows)
Carrot slices, blanched and cut into flowers
Nori

Cut the hotdog in half. Slice the cut end (2/3 the length of the hotdog) 3 times, rotate 45 degrees and slice 3 more times to make hair. Cook in boiling water until cooked through. With a small skewer or pick, skewer the meatball, then the carrot, and then the head. Decorate the faces with eyes and mouths cut from nori.

Teriyaki Meatballs
Makes 4 to 6 meatballs

INGREDIENTS

½ pound of the Teriyaki Hamburgers recipe (see page 85)
¼ cup Teriyaki Sauce (see page 108 or use store-bought)

Form teriyaki hamburger into small meatballs and fry until just cooked through. Drain excess oil and add teriyaki sauce and simmer for another 30 seconds and toss so that meatballs are covered with sauce.

flying friends

Bird Musubi
with Furikake Salmon and Thai Peanut Noodles

INGREDIENTS

Rice
Nori
1 slice kamaboko
Carrot slice
Furikake Salmon (see page 110)
Thai Peanut Noodles

Shape rice using a traditional triangular musubi mold. Wrap the musubi with a strip of nori. Cut out two eyes from the kamaboko and cut out a small beak from the carrot. Arrange the beak and eyes on the musubi. Finish the eyes with two small circles punched out from the nori.

Bees

with Shrimp Tempura and Soba

INGREDIENTS

Rice
Yellow Color Mist
4 slices kamaboko
Nori for stripes and eyes
Shrimp Tempura (see page 113)
Soba (see page 122)

Form rice into oblong musubis (or use musubi mold). Spray with yellow Color Mist. From the kamaboko, cut out small circles for the bees' eyes and cut out wings using a heart-shaped cutter. Cut thin strips of nori and place on the rice to form the bees' stripes. Arrange the kamaboko wings and eyes on the bees. Then finish the kamaboko eyes with small eyes cut out from the nori.

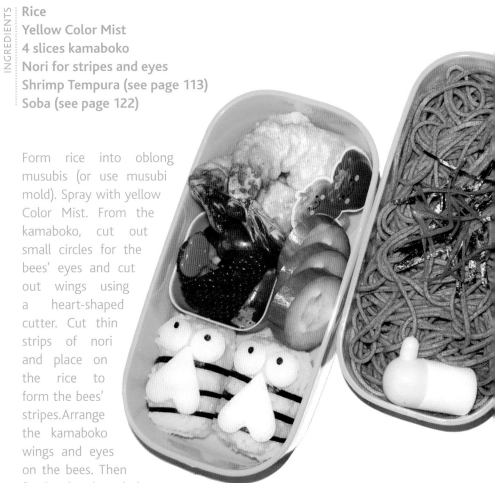

INGREDIENTS

Rice
2 jumbo pitted olives
2 carrot slices, blanched
2 slices kamaboko
Nori for stars and eyes
Teriyaki Chicken (see page 108)

Place rice in the container. Slice 2 olives in half. Use 3 of the halves as the blackbird bodies and arrange on the rice. Thinly slice the other half to make 2 wings for each bird. From the carrot, cut out 3 small triangle beaks for the birds and 6 V-shaped feet. Arrange on the birds. Cut out small circle eyes from the kamaboko and place them on the birds. Finish the eyes with small nori circles, and punch out stars to decorate the rice.

INGREDIENTS

Rice
4 slices uzumaki (steamed fish cake with a spiral pattern)
1 slice bologna
Nori
Furikake Chicken Drumettes (see page 101)

Use a flower-shaped musubi mold or cookie cutter to form rice. Thinly slice 4 slices of the uzumaki and place on the rice for wings. From the bologna, cut out 2 circles for the eyes and place on the butterfly. Cut out the antennae, mouth, and eyes from the nori and arrange on the butterfly.

Chicks
with Shrimp Spring Rolls and
Vietnamese Vermicelli Noodle Salad

INGREDIENTS

Vietnamese Vermicelli Noodle Salad (see page 125)
1 egg, beaten
2 slices kamaboko
Nori for eyes
Carrot slice for beak
Shrimp Spring Rolls (see page 112)

Place the noodles into the container. Cook the beaten egg in a small nonstick pan on low heat. Flip the omelet once and set on the side to cool. Using a fluted circle cutter, cut out two chicks from the egg and place on the noodles. Out of the kamaboko, cut 4 small circles for the chicks' eyes. Arrange the eyes on the chicks and finish the eyes with the nori cutouts. From the carrot, cut 2 small triangles for the beaks.

Chick Hamburger Stew

INGREDIENTS

Hamburger Stew (see page 83)
Rice
1 slice bologna
1 slice cheddar cheese
1 carrot slice, blanched
Nori for eyes

In a bird- or heart-shaped plate, place Hamburger Stew and rice. Cut a circle out of the bologna for the eye and place on the rice. Out of the cheese, cut a smaller circle for the inner eye of the chick and a large half-circle for the wing. Place the cheese shapes on the plate. Finish the chick's eye with a circle cut out of the nori. Cut a beak and flower out of the carrot and place on chick to complete.

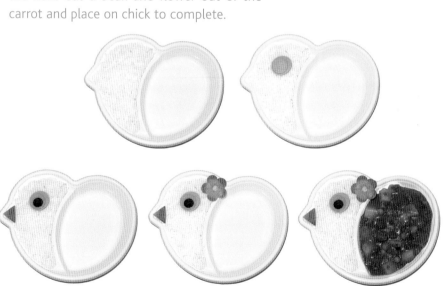

INGREDIENTS

¼ pound of Hamburger recipe (see page 82)
Rice
5 slices kamaboko plus a cross slice of only the pink part for the spots
Nori for eyes
Carrot slice, blanched

Form hamburger into 1 large patty and 2 small patties. Cook hamburger until cooked through. Place rice in the container and arrange hamburgers.

With the kamaboko, cut 2 slices for the mommy ladybug. Trim the ends (see picture) and place on the hamburger. Cut two small kamaboko circles to fit the two small hamburger patties. Cut a small notch so that it will look like wings, then place on the hamburger. From the pink part of the kamaboko, cut out spots for the ladybugs and arrange. Then cut out circles from the white part of the kamaboko to make the eyes. Finish the eyes with small circles punched out from the nori and placed on ladybugs.

Decorate the rice with small flowers cut from the carrot.

INGREDIENTS

Rice
1 egg, beaten
1 slice bologna
2 slices kamaboko
Nori for eyes
Pork Gyoza (see page 92)

Place rice into the container. Cook the beaten egg in a nonstick pan on low heat. Flip the omelet once and cool. Cut the omelet with an owl-shaped cutter, then place it on the rice.

From the bologna, cut out 2 circles for the owl's eyes, 2 ears, a beak, and 2 wings using the owl cutter (see picture) and arrange on the owl. From the kamaboko, cut out 2 smaller circles and a teardrop shape for the owl's stomach. Place the cut kamaboko on the owl and finish the eyes with eyes cut from the nori.

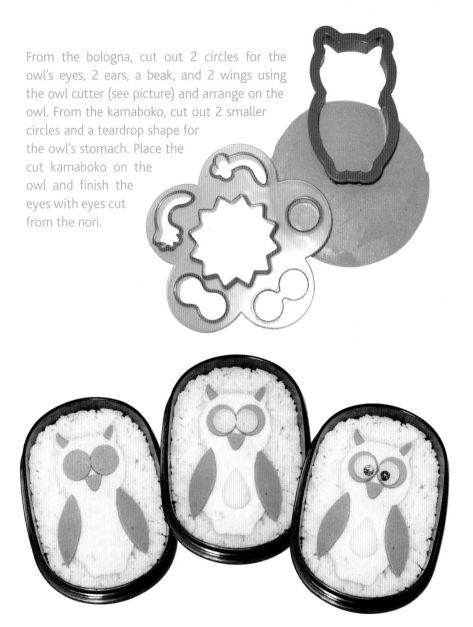

Owl SPAM® Musubi
with Fish Cake Tamago

INGREDIENTS

Rice
1 (¼-inch) slice of SPAM®
Nori
2 slices kamaboko
1 slice bologna
Fish Cake Tamago (see page 134)

Using a nigiri sushi mold, make 3 musubis. Cut SPAM® to fit the rice and pan-fry until cooked. Place the SPAM® on the rice. Wrap the SPAM® musubi with small strips of nori. Cut 6 eyes out of the kamaboko and 3 beaks out of the pink part of the kamaboko and arrange on the musubi. Cut 6 smaller circles out of the bologna for the inner part of the owl's eyes. Place bologna circles on the owl and finish with eyes punched out of nori.

furry friends

Bear Beef Stew

INGREDIENTS

Beef Stew (see page 79)
Rice
2 steamed broccoli florets
1 slice bologna
1 slice mozzarella cheese
Nori for eyes

Place stew and rice in an animal-shaped plate. Place the broccoli florets on the plate as the ears. From the bologna, cut two large circles for the eyes, one small oval for the nose, and a crescent shape for the mouth. Place the bologna shapes on the stew. For the eyes, cut two small circles out of the mozzarella, and finish with two smaller circles cut from the nori.

Bear Musubi
with Misoyaki Chicken and Citrus Soba Salad

INGREDIENTS

Rice
Furikake
1 slice kamaboko
Nori
Misoyaki Chicken (see page 105)
Citrus Soba Salad (see page 118)

Mix the rice with furikake, then shape using a bear musubi mold or cookie cutter. Cut 2 circles out of the kamaboko for the eyes and place on the bear. Cut two circles out of the nori and trim one end of each circle to make ears. Then cut out a nose and mouth, and punch out small circles for the eyes from the nori. Arrange the nori on the bear.

INGREDIENTS

Garlic Chicken Fried Rice (see page 102)
4 slices kamaboko
Nori for eyes and nose

Place fried rice in an animal-shaped bowl. Out of the kamaboko, cut 2 large circles for the eyes, 1 small oval for the nose, and a crescent shape for the mouth. Place the kamaboko shapes on the fried rice. Cut eyes and a nose out of the nori to finish.

Bunny and Bear
Teriyaki SPAM® Musubi
with Chikuwa Hotdogs

INGREDIENTS

Rice
2 (¼-inch) slices of SPAM®
Teriyaki Sauce (see page 108 or use store-bought)
Nori
Chikuwa Hotdogs (see page 128)

With bunny- and bear-shaped rice molds or cookie cutters, form musubis. Use the mold or cutter to cut the bunny and bear shapes out of the SPAM®. Cook the SPAM® in the Teriyaki Sauce and place on the musubis. Wrap with small strips of nori.

INGREDIENTS

Rice
Nori
Carrot slice, blanched
Korean Chicken (see page 104)
Sesame Broccoli (see page 132)

Shape the rice using a cat-shaped musubi mold or cookie cutter. From the nori, cut out 3 small ovals for the ears and nose and 6 small strips for the whiskers. Punch out eyes from the nori. Arrange the nori on the cat. Cut out a flower from the carrot and place on the cat.

Croquette Dog
with Teriyaki Hamburgers

INGREDIENTS

Rice
1 croquette (store-bought)
2 olives
1 slice kamaboko
Nori for eyes
Carrot slices, blanched
Teriyaki Hamburgers (see page 85)

Place rice into the container. Cook the croquette as directed on the package, then place on the rice. Cut 2 olives in half and use 3 of the halves as the dog's ears and nose. Cut 2 circles out of the kamaboko for the eyes, and finish with 2 small circles punched out from the nori. Arrange the olives and eyes on the croquette. From the carrots, cut out 2 flowers and arrange on the rice.

Croquette Lion
with Chicken Yakisoba and Shoyu Hotdog

INGREDIENTS

Chicken Yakisoba (see page 117)
1 croquette (store-bought)
2 olives
1 slice kamaboko
Nori
Rice
Shoyu Hotdog (see page 133)

Place yakisoba into the container. Cook the croquette as directed on the package. Place the croquette on the noodles. Cut 2 olives in half and use 3 of the halves as the lion's ears and nose. Cut 2 circles from the kamaboko for the eyes, then punch out eyes from the nori to finish the eyes. Arrange the eyes, ears, and nose on the lion.

To make the happy-face musubi, form a musubi out of rice. Take a strip of nori and punch a happy face on the nori using the nori punch. Wrap nori around musubi.

Hotdog Sushi Bear

Sushi Rice (recipe follows)
2 cooked hotdogs
Nori

Fill a sushi mold halfway with rice, and place the hotdog in the center (see picture). Top off with more rice, then press down with the top part of the mold. Un-mold the sushi roll and wrap with a sheet of nori. Cut the sushi roll into 8 slices. From the leftover hotdog, cut thin slices for the bears' ears. Decorate each sushi slice with the hotdog ears and noses, and nori eyes and noses.

Sushi Rice for Kids
Makes 2 rolls

INGREDIENTS

2 cups rice (makes 4 cups cooked)
2 tablespoons Japanese rice vinegar
2 tablespoons sugar
1 teaspoon salt

Wash rice until water runs clear, and cook with 2 cups of water. Combine the vinegar, sugar, and salt in a small bowl and mix well. When rice is done let steam for 15 minutes longer. Next, fold the vinegar mixture into the rice, and let cool before making sushi. Cover with a damp towel so that the rice doesn't become dry.

Mandoo Mice

INGREDIENTS

3 Fried Mandoo (see page 91)
1 slice bologna
1 slice cheddar cheese
3 slices kamaboko
Nori for eyes
Celery for tails

1. Place the mandoo in the container.

2. Cut out 3 large circles for the ears from the bologna.

3. From the cheese, cut out 3 teardrop shapes (with the pointed tip cut off) for the inner ears.

   Also cut a cheese-shaped piece. With the cheese-shaped piece, take a small circle cutter and punch out holes and place it on the rice.

   Cut 3 circles from the kamaboko for the eyes. Arrange the ears and eyes on the mice. To finish the eyes, cut circles from the nori and punch out the inside of the circle, then place nori eyes on the kamaboko.

4. Cut thin slivers of celery for the tails.

Mice

with Corned Beef Hash and Potato Macaroni Salad

INGREDIENTS

Rice
1 hotdog, cooked
3 olives
2 slices kamaboko
Nori
1 slice cheddar cheese
Corned Beef Hash (see page 81)
Potato Macaroni Salad (see page 131)

Place rice in the container. Cut 6 slices from the hotdog for the mice's ears, and 3 small circles for their noses. Cut three olives in half and use the bottom halves as the heads. Cut 6 small circles from the kamaboko for the eyes. Then punch out eyes from the nori and place on the kamaboko. Arrange the mice on the rice. Then cut three cheese wedges from the cheddar and punch small holes in the cheese.

Pandas
with Chicken Karaage

INGREDIENTS

Rice
Nori
Chicken Karaage (see page 98)

Shape the rice using a bear-shaped musubi mold or cookie cutter. From the nori, cut out 9 circles for the outer part of the eyes, ears, and mouth. Take 4 of the circles and punch a small circle with the nori punch to form the outer part of the eye. Place the eyes on the pandas. Then place the small nori circles that were punched out on the inner part of the eyes so that they resemble a pandas' eyes. Trim off a little of 4 remaining circles to form the ears. Cut the last circle in half to form the mouths. Punch out 2 smaller circles from the nori for the pandas' noses.

Missy Mouse
with Asian Turkey Burgers
and Chinese Salad with Crispy Noodles

INGREDIENTS

Rice
1 slice bologna
1 slice cheddar cheese
2 slices kamaboko
Carrot slices, blanched
Nori for eyes
Asian Turkey Bugers (see page 96)
Chinese Salad with Crispy Noodles (see page 129)

1. Place rice into a mouse-shaped container (or use a mouse-shaped cookie cutter to mold rice). From the bologna, cut out two small circles for eyes and two large circles for the ears. Cut away a little of the bottom of the large bologna circles to form ears (see picture).

2. Cut out two crescents from the cheese to form the inside of the ears. Cut two small circles from sliced kamaboko for the inner eyes.

3. Then cut a flower and nose out of the carrot. To assemble (see picture) place the bologna eyes and ears and carrot nose on the rice. Add the cheese inner ears and kamaboko eyes. Finish with the carrot flower and nori eyes.

Rabbit Musubis

with Kalbi and Bean Sprout Namul

INGREDIENTS

Rice
Furikake
1 slice bologna
2 slices kamaboko
Nori for eyes and nose
Kalbi (see page 84)
Bean Sprout Namul (see page 126)

Mix the rice with furikake, then shape the rice using a rabbit-shaped musubi mold or cookie cutter. Cut out 4 ears from the bologna. Then cut out 4 small circles for the rabbits' eyes from the kamaboko. Arrange the ears and eyes on rabbits. Finish the rabbits with eyes and noses punched out from nori.

INGREDIENTS

Rice
1 olive
1 slice kamaboko
Nori for eyes
Tonkatsu (see page 94)

Form the rice into an oblong musubi (or use rice mold). Slice the olive in half and place one half on the musubi for the head. With the other half of the olive, make 3 thin lengthwise slices for the ears and tail, and arrange on the sheep. Cut eyes from the kamaboko and finish with small circles punched out from the nori. Cover the top of the sheep's head and ears with a little rice.

Tiger
with Bacon-and-Corn Chowder

INGREDIENTS

Bacon-and-Corn Chowder (see page 87)
Rice
1 slice bologna
1 slice cheddar cheese
Nori for eyes

Place the chowder and rice in an animal-shaped plate. From the bologna, cut 2 small circles for the eyes, a small oval for the nose, and stripes . for the tiger. Using the cheese, cut out a mouth for the tiger. Place the bologna eyes, nose, and stripes on the tiger. Then add the mouth, and finish the eyes with two small circles cut from nori.

scrumptious sammies

2 slices white bread
Your favorite deli meat or sandwich filling
1 slice bologna
1 slice cheddar cheese
Nori for eyes and mouth
Heart cake decorations

Using a circle cutter, cut out the bread and deli meat (or your choice of filling). Assemble the sandwich and place into the container.

1. Then use the rabbit cutter to cut out 2 rabbit shapes from the bologna and cheese.

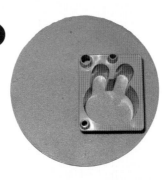

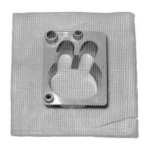

2. Flip the cutter over to cut off all the ears from the bologna and cheese shapes. Save 2 of the cheese ears to make the girl's pigtails. Then use the bottom of the rabbit cutter to cut the two oval cheese shapes to use as the top part of their hair (see pictures).

3. To make the girl and boy, place the oval-shaped bologna on the sandwich. Top with the cheese hair and pigtails (for the girl).

4. Add nori eyes and mouth, and finish the girl with two cake decoration hearts for her hair.

Alien Kālua BBQ Pork Sandwich

INGREDIENTS

2 slices cheddar cheese
1 slice mozzarella cheese
Small crusty roll
Nori for eyes
3 ounces BBQ Kālua Pork (see page 89)
2 decorative picks for antennae

Use a large daisy cutter to cut 1 slice of cheddar cheese for the inside of the sandwich. Then with the other slice, cut out two arms and a pair of eyeglasses.

With the mozzarella cheese, cut out the small circle eyes, an oval nose, and a half moon-shaped mouth.

To assemble, cut the roll in half. On the bottom half place daisy-shaped cheese, then BBQ Kālua Pork, and top with the other half of the roll. On top of the roll place the eyeglasses with the small circle eyes on top of it. Finish eyes with eyes punched out from nori. Add the nose, mouth, arms, and antennae.

Child's Name Sandwich

INGREDIENTS

2 slices bread
Your favorite sandwich filling
1 slice cheddar cheese for name

Cut out bread with your choice of cutter.

Cut your child's name out of the cheddar cheese using the alphabet cutters. If your child has more letters than the space provided, either use his/her nickname or use a larger cutter for the sandwich.

Assemble the sandwich and place the child's name across it.

Daisy Sandwich

INGREDIENTS
....

  2 slices bread
  Your favorite deli meat or sandwich filling
  Fruit snacks

Cut the bread and deli meat with a daisy-shaped cutter. Assemble the sandwich and skewer it using a decorative pick with fruit snacks.

Hamburger Man

INGREDIENTS

1 slice cheddar cheese
1 slice mozzarella cheese
1 slice bologna
Nori for eyes
Small crusty roll
1 small cooked Hamburger to fit bun size (see page 82)

From the cheddar cheese, cut a large daisy shape and an oval nose.

From the mozzarella, cut two small circle eyes.

From the bologna, cut a medium-sized circle for the hamburger's tongue and two smaller circles for the eyes.

Cut out two eyes from the nori using the nori punch.

To assemble, cut the roll in half. Place the cooked hamburger on the bottom half of the roll, then the daisy cheese, and the medium-sized circle bologna on one edge of the cheese so that it looks like a tongue when the top of the roll is placed over it. Decorate top of the roll with the two small mozzarella circles placed on top of the bologna circles to make the eyes. Then place the two nori cutouts on the eyes to finish. Finally add the hamburger man's nose.

INGREDIENTS
....

4 slices bread
Your choice of deli meat and cheese for the sandwich filling
1 slice cheddar cheese

Using the heart and butterfly cutters, cut out bread, deli meat, and cheese. With the cutter, cut 7 small hearts out of the cheddar cheese. Assemble the sandwich, then top with the small cheddar hearts.

Heart and Flower Sandwich Skewers

INGREDIENTS

4 slices bread (2 slices white, 2 slices wheat)
Your favorite deli meat or sandwich filling
4 slices cheddar cheese
Fruit snacks and goldfish crackers
4 decorative picks

Use cutters to cut out 8 (4 white, 4 wheat) flowers and 8 (4 white, 4 wheat) hearts out of the bread. Then cut 8 flowers and 8 hearts from the cheddar and deli meat. Assemble the sandwich on a skewer in the following order: white bread, cheddar, deli meat, wheat bread, white bread, cheddar, deli meat, wheat bread, and then the fruit snack at the end.

Mouse Sandwich

INGREDIENTS

2 slices white bread
Your favorite deli meat or sandwich filling
1 slice bologna
1 slice cheddar cheese
Nori for eyes

1. Use a small circle cutter to cut the bread (4 circles) and deli meat for the ears. Then use a large circle cutter to cut the bread (2 circles) and deli meat for the head. Assemble sandwich and place in container.

1

2. Then, out of the bologna, cut 2 medium-sized circles for the ears, 2 small circles for the eyes, and a small oval for the nose. From the cheese, cut out 2 teardrop shapes (cut off the pointed end) for the ears, 2 circles for the eyes, and a small crescent shape for the mouth. Assemble the mouse (see picture) and finish the eyes with two small circles punched out from the nori.

2

Keiki Sandwich

INGREDIENTS

2 slices of your favorite bread
Your favorite deli meat or sandwich filling
1 slice mozzarella cheese
1 slice cheddar cheese
1 slice bologna
Nori for eyes

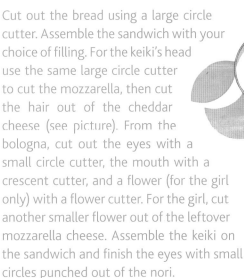

Cut out the bread using a large circle cutter. Assemble the sandwich with your choice of filling. For the keiki's head use the same large circle cutter to cut the mozzarella, then cut the hair out of the cheddar cheese (see picture). From the bologna, cut out the eyes with a small circle cutter, the mouth with a crescent cutter, and a flower (for the girl only) with a flower cutter. For the girl, cut another smaller flower out of the leftover mozzarella cheese. Assemble the keiki on the sandwich and finish the eyes with small circles punched out of the nori.

Char Siu Bunny Bao

INGREDIENTS

1 slice bologna
1 slice cheddar cheese
Nori for eyes
2 slices of apple for ears
Hoisin Mayo (see page 57)
Chinese steamed bao
Char siu, thinly sliced
Green onion brush for hair
Thinly sliced green onions (optional)

Cut the eyes out of bologna. Then cut the inside of the ears and the nose out of the cheese. With a scissors cut out two circles for the eyes and use the nori punch to punch out a hole in each circle.

To assemble, spread a little of the Hoisin Mayo on the inside of bun. Then add in sliced char siu and green onions. Place in container then add on the bologna and cheese eyes and nose. Finish the eyes with the nori eyes. Place the apples slightly in the bun for the ears and complete with the cheese cutout for the inner ears. Cut a 2-inch piece from the bottom white part of the green onion. Thinly slice the top half of the cut piece until it looks like the picture. Insert green onion brush between the ears.

Roast Pork Mouse Bao

INGREDIENTS

1 slice bologna
1 slice cheddar cheese
Nori for eyes
Hoisin Mayo (recipe follows)
Chinese steamed bao
Chinese roast pork, thinly sliced
Thinly sliced green onions (optional)

Cut the ears, eyes, and nose out of bologna. Then cut the insides of the eyes and ears out of the cheese. With the nori punch, cut out the eyes for the mouse.

To assemble, spread a little of the Hoisin Mayo on the inside of bun. Then add the sliced roast pork and green onions. Place in the container then add the bologna and cheese eyes, nose, and ears. Finish the eyes with the nori punchouts.

Hoisin Mayo

INGREDIENTS

¼ cup mayonnaise
2 teaspoons hoisin sauce
¼ teaspoon sesame oil

Combine all ingredients and mix well.

Sun-wich

INGREDIENTS

2 slices wheat bread
Your favorite deli meat or sandwich filling
1 slice cheddar cheese
1 slice mozzarella cheese
Nori for eyes and mouth

Cut out the bread using a circle cutter. Assemble the sandwich with your favorite filling. Cut 2 suns out of the cheddar cheese using a sun-shaped cutter and place on the sandwich. Cut 4 small circles for the eyes and a bow (for the girl sun) out of the mozzarella cheese and place on sandwich. Cut 4 large circle eyes out of the nori and punch a small hole in each of the eyes. Punch out a mouth from the nori for each. Finish the sun with the nori eyes and mouth.

rice 'n more

Dinosaur
with Teriyaki Steak

INGREDIENTS

Rice
1 egg, beaten
Carrot slices, blanched
Nori for eye
Teriyaki Steak (see page 86)

Place rice into the container. Cook the beaten egg in a nonstick pan on low heat. Flip the omelet once and cool. Cut the omelet with a dinosaur-shaped cutter, then place the dinosaur on the rice. From the carrot, cut out 1 star to decorate the rice and several small circles for the dinosaur's body. Arrange carrot spots on the dinosaur and cut the rest of the circles in half and place on the ridge of his back. Finish the dinosaur with an eye cut from nori.

Elephant Chili

INGREDIENTS

Chili (see page 80)
Rice
Corn
1 slice bologna
1 slice cheddar cheese
Nori for eye

Using an elephant-shaped plate, place chili, rice, and corn in the compartments. From the bologna, cut out a small circle for the elephant's eye and a large crescent shape for the ear, then place the shapes on the rice. From the cheese, cut out a small crescent shape for the mouth and a half circle for the eyelid. Cut out a circle for the eye from the nori and place on the bologna circle, then finish with the cheese eyelid and mouth.

INGREDIENTS

Rice
3 jumbo-sized pitted olives
1 slice bologna
1 slice mozzarella
Homemade Chicken Breast Nuggets (see page 103)

Place rice into a fish-shaped container (or use a fish-shaped cookie cutter to mold rice).

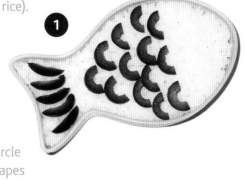

1. Slice the olives crosswise and then in half to form the scales of the fish and place on the rice. Slice an olive lengthwise and place on the rice to form the tail.

2. Out of the bologna, cut a large circle for the eye and two crescent shapes for the mouth and the fin, and place on the fish.

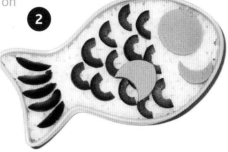

3. To finish the eye, cut a small circle out of the mozzarella for the inner eye, and cut the end off of an olive for the eyeball.

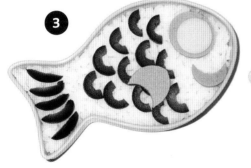

Gecko
with Mochiko Chicken and Tamago

INGREDIENTS

Rice

1 egg, beaten

3 carrot slices, blanched

1 slice kamaboko

Nori for eyes

Soybean

Black sesame seeds for bug's eyes

Place rice into the container. Cook the beaten egg in a nonstick pan on low heat. Flip the omelet once and cool.

1. Cut the omelet with a gecko-shaped cutter, then place the gecko on the rice.

2. With the carrot, cut out 2 small heart-shaped wings for the bug and several small circles for the gecko's spots. Arrange the spots on gecko and place the wings on the rice. Cut out 2 small circles from the kamaboko for the gecko's eyes.

3. Finish with eyes cut out from nori. Place the soybean on the carrot wings and finish the bug with the 2 black sesame seed eyes.

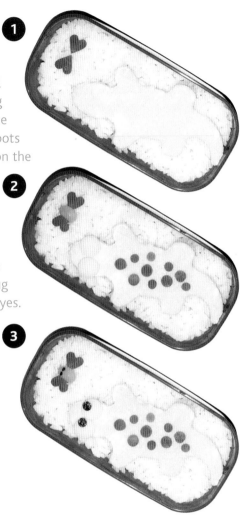

INGREDIENTS

Rice
1 slice bologna
1 slice cheddar cheese
3 carrot slices, blanched
Fried Shrimp (see page 109)
Nori for eyes and mouth
Cake decorations
1 hotdog

1. Place rice in the container. With a bear-shaped cutter, cut the head for the mermaid from the bologna. Then cut out 2 circles, 1 for the body, and cut the sides of the other circle to make arms.

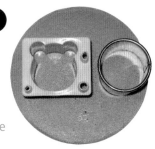

2. Using the bear cutter again, cut the hair out of the cheese (see picture).

   Cut 5 small stars and 1 heart out of the carrot. Cut the pointed end of the heart off; the rest of the heart will be used for the mermaid's tail fin.

3. Arrange the mermaid's head, hair, body, and arms on the rice. Cut the tail off the Fried Shrimp and use it as the mermaid's tail with the carrot heart as the fins. Use the carrot stars for the mermaid's top and decorate the rice with the rest of the stars. Add her nori eyes and mouth and finish her hair and belly button with the cake decorations.

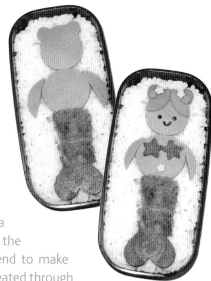

To make the hotdog octopus, cut a hotdog in half and make slits (about ⅔ the length of the hotdog) from the cut end to make tentacles. Cook in boiling water until heated through and the tentacles separate. When cool, add the nori eyes and mouth.

INGREDIENTS

Bacon and Portuguese Sausage Fried Rice (see page 88)
1 egg, beaten
3 carrot slices, blanched
1 slice kamaboko
Nori for eyes and mouth

Place fried rice into the container. Cook the beaten egg in a nonstick pan on low heat. Flip the omelet once and cool. Cut the omelet with an octopus-shaped cutter, then place the octopus on the fried rice. From the carrot, cut out several small circles for the octopus's tentacles and 2 star shapes. Place the starfishs on the rice and arrange the carrot circles on the tentacles. Cut out 2 small circles for the eyes, and a crescent shape for the mouth from the kamaboko and arrange on the octopus. Cut out the octopus's eyes and the starfishs' eyes and mouths from the nori.

INGREDIENTS

Rice
1 (¼-inch) slice SPAM®
Nori
3 slices kamaboko
Macaroni Salad (see page 130)

Using a nigiri sushi mold, make 3 musubis. Cut SPAM® to fit the rice and pan-fry until cooked. Place the SPAM® on the rice. Cut 3 sheets of nori to fit the spam musubi and wrap with the nori. Cut 6 small circles out of the kamaboko for the eyes and 6 larger half-circles for the wings. From the pink part of the kamaboko, cut 3 small triangles for the beaks. Arrange the eyes, wings, and beaks on the penguins. Finish the penguins with eyes punched out from the nori.

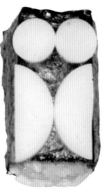

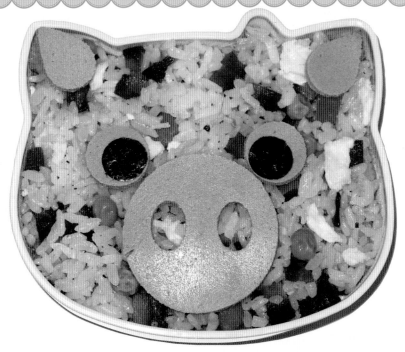

INGREDIENTS

Char Siu Fried Rice (see page 90)
1 slice bologna
Nori for eyes

Fill a cat-shaped container with the Char Siu Fried Rice. Cut 2 small circles for the pig's eyes and 2 teardrop shapes for the ears out of the bologna. Then cut a large circle shape out of the bologna, and cut 2 small ovals from the circle to form a snout. Place the cut bologna onto the fried rice and finish the eyes with 2 small circles cut from the nori.

Pumpkin Patch
with Tamago and Fried Chicken

INGREDIENTS

Rice
Furikake
3 carrot slices, blanched
2 slices kamaboko
Nori for eyes

Place rice into the container. In a small bowl mix a little rice with furikake. Using your wet fingers, place the furikake rice on top of the white rice in the container so that it looks like the ground of the pumpkin patch (see picture). From the carrot slices, cut out 3 pumpkins and arrange them on the rice. From the kamaboko, cut out 8 small circles to use as the eyes and mouths of the pumpkins. To make the mouth, cut a circle in half. Cut out a bow for the girl pumpkin from the pink part of the kamaboko. Arrange the kamaboko on the pumpkins and finish the eyes with small circles punched out from the nori.

INGREDIENTS

Rice
3 slices kamaboko
Red Color Mist
Carrot
Nori
Stuffed Salmon (see page 114)
Fish Cake Tamago (see page 134)

Dampen a snowman-shaped cookie cutter with water and place in the container. Pack rice into the cutter, then carefully remove the cutter, leaving the snowman-shaped rice. Cut a hat and scarf out of the kamaboko, and spray with red Color Mist. When the hat and scarf are dry, place them on the snowman. Cut a small sliver of carrot for the nose and place on snowman. Out of the nori, cut a strip for the hat, 2 eyes, several small circles for the mouth, and 2 buttons. Arrange the nori on the snowman to complete.

INGREDIENTS

Rice
Furikake
¼ pound of Teriyaki Hamburger recipe (see page 85)
2 tablespoons Teriyaki Sauce (see page 108 or use store-bought)
1 thin slice kamaboko
Nori for eye
2 carrot slices, blanched
Furikake Imitation Crab Noodles (see page 120)

Place rice in the container. Mix a little furikake with a small amount of rice for the ground. With wet fingers, place the furikake rice onto the white rice.

Roll the Teriyaki Hamburger into small meatballs and fry until just cooked. Drain the excess fat and add Teriyaki Sauce. Toss in the sauce and cook for a few seconds longer. Arrange the meatballs on the rice to look like a worm.

Cut out a small circle from the kamaboko for the eye. Then punch out a small circle from the nori and place on the kamaboko to finish the eye, and place on worm.

With the carrots, cut out small flowers and decorate the rice.

INGREDIENTS

Shrimp Tempura or Fried Shrimp (see page 113 or page 109)
Rice
Nori
1 slice kamaboko

To make the whale, take a cooked shrimp and pack rice around it, leaving the shrimp tail exposed. Form the musubi into a triangular shape and wrap with a sheet of nori. Cut a small circle for the eye from the white part of the kamaboko and cut a mouth from pink part of the kamaboko. Place the mouth and eye on the whale. Finish with an eye punched out from the nori.

Ice Cream
with Chicken Adobo

INGREDIENTS

Rice
Ice cream cone
Chicken Adobo (see page 97)

Form a ball of rice that will fit on the ice cream cone. Wrap the ball in plastic wrap and place it on the cone. Wrap the cone and rice in a decorative bag.

You can also replace the plain rice with fried rice or rice mixed with furikake or add cutouts made from nori.

PART II 'ONO RECIPES

Barbeque Beef
Serves 4

INGREDIENTS

1 cup shoyu
¼ cup mirin
½ cup sugar
½ cup red miso
2 tablespoons sesame oil
4 cloves garlic, minced
1 teaspoon ginger, grated
1 tablespoon toasted sesame seeds
2 tablespoons thinly sliced green onions
1½ pounds thinly sliced beef

Combine the shoyu, mirin, sugar, miso, sesame oil, garlic, ginger, sesame seeds, and green onions in a bowl and mix well. Reserve ¼ cup of marinade to brush on after cooking. Add beef and marinate for 20 to 30 minutes. Grill or pan-fry until done. Brush with extra sauce if desired.

Beef with Broccoli
Serves 4

INGREDIENTS

2 tablespoons shoyu
1 tablespoon sake or sherry
1 tablespoon + 1 teaspoon cornstarch
2 teaspoons sugar
¼ teaspoon grated ginger
1 clove garlic, minced
½ teaspoon pepper
½ pound beef, thinly sliced
1 pound broccoli, cut into bite-sized pieces
1 tablespoon oil
½ cup chicken broth
1 teaspoon salt

In a bowl combine shoyu, sherry, 2 teaspoons cornstarch, sugar, ginger, garlic, and pepper; mix well. Toss beef in marinade and let sit for 10 minutes. In the meantime, boil water and blanch broccoli for 10 to 15 seconds; drain well. Add oil to a large pan on high heat. Brown beef in the pan then add broccoli; mix well. Add chicken broth mixed with 1 teaspoon of cornstarch to thicken and ½ teaspoon of salt.

Beef Stew

Serves 6 to 8

INGREDIENTS

3 pounds boneless beef chuck, cut into 1-inch cubes
Salt and pepper to season
½ cup flour
4 tablespoons extra-virgin olive oil
1 cup water
2 (14-ounce) cans chicken broth
2 (14-ounce) cans beef broth
1 (14.5-ounce) can sliced stewed tomatoes
1 (6-ounce) can tomato paste
2 bay leaves
3 cloves garlic, minced
2 large carrots, cut into 1-inch pieces
1 medium-sized onion, cut into 1-inch pieces
3 stalks celery, cut into 1-inch pieces
3 russet potatoes, cut into 1-inch cubes
Cornstarch and water for thickening if needed (1:1 ratio)

Lightly season beef with salt and pepper. Dust seasoned beef with flour. Brown in a large pot with oil on medium-high heat. Add water and bring to a boil. Scrape brown bits off the bottom of the pot with a wooden spoon. Add chicken broth, beef broth, stewed tomatoes, tomato paste, bay leaves, and garlic. Bring to a rolling boil and cook for 30 minutes, stirring occasionally. Skim and discard any fat that has accumulated at the top. Add carrots, onion, and celery. Bring to a rolling boil and cook for another 15 minutes. Add potatoes, bring to a rolling boil, and cook for another 15 minutes. If stew needs to be thickened, make a slurry out of cornstarch and water (1:1 ratio), and add a little at a time until thickened to desired consistency.

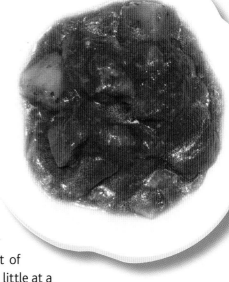

Chili
Serves 4

1¼ pounds lean ground beef
3 slices bacon, cut into ¼-inch pieces
½ pound Portuguese sausage, cut into ½-inch pieces
3 cloves garlic, minced
1 small onion, diced into ¼-inch pieces
1 teaspoon salt
½ teaspoon pepper
½ teaspoon oregano
1 tablespoon chili powder
1 (14.5-ounce) can stewed tomatoes
1 (15.5-ounce) can chili beans
1 (14-ounce) can crushed tomatoes

In a pot, brown hamburger and bacon on medium-high heat until cooked. Add Portuguese sausage, garlic, onion, salt, pepper, oregano, and chili powder and cook until onion is soft. Add stewed tomatoes, chili beans, and crushed tomatoes and bring to a boil. Lower heat to medium and simmer for 1 hour, stirring occasionally. Taste and adjust seasoning if necessary.

Corned Beef Hash
Serves 4

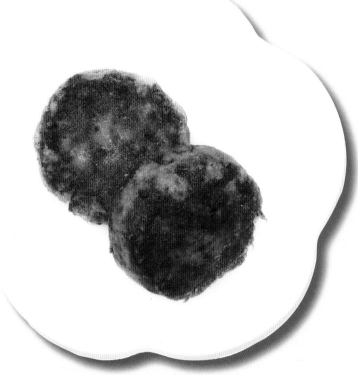

1 russet potato, diced into ¼-inch cubes
1 can corned beef
1 egg, beaten
2 tablespoons thinly sliced green onions
2 tablespoons minced onion
¼ teaspoon pepper
Flour
Oil for frying

Cook diced potatoes in boiling water until soft and well cooked. Drain well and cool. Combine the corned beef, egg, green onions, onion, pepper, and cooled potatoes in a large bowl. Form into small patties and lightly dust with flour. Cook in a heated pan with oil until golden and cooked through.

Hamburger
Serves 6

2 pounds ground beef
2 eggs
½ cup bread crumbs
½ cup mayonnaise
1 tablespoon garlic salt
1 teaspoon pepper
2 teaspoons onion powder

Combine all ingredients. Form into patties and cook until cooked through.

Hamburger Stew
Serves 5

1½ pounds ground beef
1 (26-ounce) can condensed cream of mushroom soup
1 (14.5-ounce) can low-sodium beef broth
1 (14.5-ounce) can stewed tomatoes, drained
2 large russet potatoes, cubed into ½-inch pieces
½ teaspoon salt
¼ teaspoon pepper
½ pound frozen peas and carrots

In a large pot, brown ground beef. Add mushroom soup, beef broth, stewed tomatoes, potatoes, salt, and pepper. Simmer for 15 to 20 minutes on medium heat until potatoes are soft. Add frozen peas and carrots, then cook for another 10 minutes.

Kalbi
Serves 4

¾ cup shoyu
¾ cup brown sugar
1½ teaspoons sesame oil
2 cloves garlic, minced
1 thumb-sized piece ginger, lightly crushed
1 teaspoon sesame seeds
4 stalks green onion, cut into 1-inch pieces
2 teaspoons bourbon
2 pounds thinly sliced short ribs

Combine shoyu, brown sugar, sesame oil, garlic, ginger, sesame seeds, green onions, and bourbon in a bowl; mix until all of the sugar dissolves. Reserve ¼ cup of marinade for basting. Place short ribs into a self-sealing bag and pour the rest of the marinade all over it. Take air out of the bag, seal, and place in the refrigerator to marinate overnight. Cook over a hot grill or broil (basting occasionally) until done. Garnish with sesame seeds and sliced green onions.

Teriyaki Hamburgers
Serves 6

2 pounds ground beef
2 eggs
3 stalks green onion, thinly sliced
½ cup bread crumbs
½ cup mayonnaise
1 teaspoon pepper
2 teaspoons onion powder
1 teaspoon salt
2 tablespoons or more Teriyaki Sauce for basting (see page 108 or use store-bought)

Combine all ingredients. Form into patties and cook until cooked through. Baste with Teriyaki Sauce.

Teriyaki Steak
Serves 4

INGREDIENTS
....

1½ pounds steak
2¼ cups Teriyaki Sauce (see page 108 or use store-bought)
Green onions and sesame seeds to garnish

Marinate steak overnight in 2 cups Teriyaki Sauce. Grill or broil until desired doneness. Brush with the reserved ¼ cup Teriyaki Sauce. Slice to serve and garnish with green onions and sesame seeds.

Bacon-and-Corn Chowder
Serves 4

PORK

½ pound bacon, sliced into ¼-inch pieces
½ medium onion, cut into ¼-inch pieces
3 cups milk
1 (14.75 ounce) can cream corn
1 (10.75 ounce) can condensed cream of chicken soup
2 russet potatoes, diced into ½-inch cubes
1 cup frozen corn kernels
1 teaspoon salt
¼ teaspoon pepper

In a large pot, cook bacon until crisp. Add onions and cook until soft. Then add milk, cream corn, cream of chicken soup, potatoes, frozen corn, salt, and pepper. Bring to a boil, then lower heat and simmer for about 30 minutes until potatoes are soft and chowder is thickened.

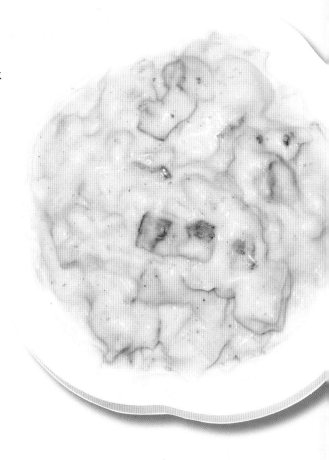

Bacon and Portuguese Sausage Fried Rice

Serves 4

INGREDIENTS

2 eggs, beaten
6 ounces bacon, cut into ¼-inch pieces
4 ounces Portuguese sausage, cut into ¼-inch pieces
6 cups day-old cooked rice
1½ tablespoons oyster sauce
¾ teaspoon garlic salt
¼ teaspoon pepper
½ cup frozen peas and carrots

Scramble beaten eggs and reserve. In a large pan, cook bacon until almost crisp then add Portuguese sausage and cook until browned. Add rice, oyster sauce, garlic salt, pepper, and peas and carrots. Mix until seasonings are evenly distributed throughout the rice. Remove from heat and fold in scrambled eggs.

BBQ Kālua Pork
Serves 4

2 pounds heated Kālua Pork (see page 93)
¾ to 1 cup of your favorite barbeque sauce (store-bought)

Drain excess liquid from pork, then toss pork with barbeque sauce. Serve on crusty rolls.

Char Siu Fried Rice

Serves 4

2 eggs, beaten
2 tablespoons oil
½ pound char siu, cut into ¼-inch pieces
1 clove garlic, minced
6 cups day-old cooked rice
1 teaspoon salt
½ teaspoon pepper
1 tablespoon shoyu
½ cup frozen peas and carrots

Scramble the two beaten eggs and reserve. In a large pan (or wok) on medium-high heat, add oil, char siu, and garlic; cook until heated through. Add rice, salt, pepper, and shoyu; mix until rice is heated through and there are no clumps. Add peas and carrots; cook for another minute. Remove from heat and fold in scrambled eggs.

Fried Mandoo
Serves 4

INGREDIENTS

½ pound ground pork
¼ pound ground beef
½ teaspoon minced garlic
½ tablespoon thinly sliced chives
½ tablespoon sesame oil
½ teaspoon salt
¼ teaspoon pepper
1 egg, beaten and divided
About 24 mandoo wrappers
Oil for frying

Combine ground pork, ground beef, garlic, chives, sesame oil, salt, pepper, and ¾ of the beaten egg in a bowl; mix well. Place a mandoo wrapper on your workspace and brush the outside edges with a little of the remaining beaten egg. In the center of the wrapper, place 1 tablespoon of the meat mixture, and fold the wrapper over so that it looks like a half moon. Crimp the edges of the wrapper to seal. To cook, heat enough oil to deep-fry the mandoo. Mandoo is done when the outside is golden and crisp. Serve with Mandoo Dipping Sauce (recipe follows).

Mandoo Dipping Sauce

INGREDIENTS

¼ cup shoyu
¼ cup seasoned Japanese rice vinegar
1 tablespoon thinly sliced green onions
2 teaspoons sesame oil
1 teaspoon toasted sesame seeds

Combine all ingredients and mix well.

Pork Gyoza
Serves 3

INGREDIENTS

½ pound ground pork
¼ teaspoon finely minced garlic
1 tablespoon thinly sliced green onions
½ teaspoon salt
¼ teaspoon pepper
1 egg, beaten and divided
16 gyoza wrappers
1 tablespoon oil
½ cup water

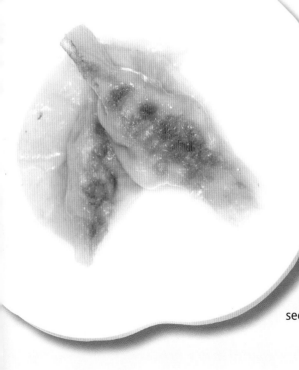

Combine the ground pork, garlic, green onions, salt, pepper, and half of the beaten egg in a bowl and mix well. Place a gyoza wrapper on your workspace and brush the outside edges with a little of the beaten egg. In the center of the wrapper, place 1 tablespoon of the meat mixture and fold the wrapper over so that it looks like a half moon. Crimp the edges of the wrapper to seal. To cook, heat a small nonstick pan (with a lid) to medium-high, add a teaspoon of oil, and fry one side of gyoza until browned. Add about 1/2 cup water to the pan and cover immediately. Let steam for 4 to 5 minutes until all the water has evaporated. Remove the lid and let cook for another 30 seconds to crisp on one side.

Slow Cooker Kālua Pork
Serves 8 to 10

INGREDIENTS

4- to 5-pound pork shoulder
2 tablespoons Liquid Smoke
2 tablespoons Hawaiian salt
2 large ti leaves
1 cup water

Rub pork all over with Liquid Smoke and Hawaiian salt, then wrap in 2 clean ti leaves. Place pork in slow cooker, add 1 cup of water to the bottom of the slow cooker and cover. Cook on high for 5 to 6 hours until the pork is easily shredded. When done, remove pork from slow cooker, discard ti leaves, and shred pork by hand or by using two forks. Sprinkle shredded pork with a little of the cooking liquid to season.

Tonkatsu
Serves 4

INGREDIENTS

1½ pounds pork cutlet
Garlic salt and pepper to taste
1 cup flour
3 eggs
1 tablespoon water
1 teaspoon sugar
3 cups panko (Japanese bread crumbs)
Oil for frying

Pat pork cutlets dry with a paper towel, then season with garlic salt and pepper. Lightly dredge pork in flour and shake off excess. Beat the 3 eggs with water and sugar to make an egg wash. Dredge floured pork in egg and finally in panko. Deep-fry in oil until golden and cooked through. Serve with Katsu Sauce (recipe follows).

Katsu Sauce

INGREDIENTS

1 cup ketchup
1 tablespoon Worcestershire sauce
⅛ teaspoon pepper

Combine all ingredients and mix well.

Wontons
Serves 4 as a side

INGREDIENTS

½ pound ground pork
¼ teaspoon finely minced garlic
½ teaspoon sesame oil
½ teaspoon salt
¼ teaspoon pepper
1 egg, beaten and divided
16 wonton wrappers

Combine ground pork, garlic, sesame oil, salt, pepper, and half of the beaten egg in a bowl; mix well. Place a wonton wrapper on your workspace and brush the outside edges with a little of the beaten egg. In the center of the wrapper, place 1 tablespoon of the meat mixture and fold one corner over to the opposite corner to form a triangle (see picture). Bring together the bottom corners of the wonton and overlap, then seal the two corners together with a little of the egg wash. Deep-fry until golden brown and cooked through.

Asian Turkey Burgers
Serves 4

POULTRY

1 pound lean ground turkey
1 egg
1 tablespoon thinly sliced green onions
2 tablespoons panko (Japanese bread crumbs)
½ teaspoon minced garlic
1 teaspoon sesame oil
1 teaspoon salt
½ teaspoon pepper
2 teaspoons mayonnaise
½ cup cornstarch
Oil for frying

Mix together ground turkey, egg, green onions, panko, garlic, sesame oil, salt, pepper, and mayonnaise. Form into small patties (mix should make 16 burgers). Lightly dust with cornstarch and pan-fry with a little oil until cooked through. Serve with Dipping Sauce (recipe follows).

Dipping Sauce

INGREDIENTS

¼ cup shoyu
¼ cup seasoned Japanese rice vinegar
1 teaspoon sesame oil
1 tablespoon thinly sliced green onions

Combine all ingredients and mix well.

Chicken Adobo
Serves 4 to 6

INGREDIENTS

3 pounds skinless chicken (any part, with or without the bone)
½ cup garlic, chopped
½ cup shoyu
¼ cup white vinegar
¼ cup water
1 tablespoon brown sugar
4 bay leaves
1 teaspoon crushed peppercorns

Add chicken, garlic, shoyu, white vinegar, water, brown sugar, bay leaves, and peppercorns to a large pot. Bring to a boil on high heat, then reduce to medium and cook for about 15 minutes. Reduce heat to low and heat a nonstick sauté pan on medium heat. In batches, remove chicken from pot and brown on all sides in sauté pan. Return chicken to pot and simmer until tender, about another 15 minutes.

Chicken Karaage
Serves 4

1½ pounds boneless skinless chicken thighs
¼ cup shoyu
¼ teaspoon finely grated ginger
2 large cloves garlic, minced
1 teaspoon sugar
½ teaspoon salt
¼ teaspoon pepper
2 tablespoons mirin
¼ cup flour mixed with ¾ cup cornstarch
Oil for frying
Lemon slice for garnish

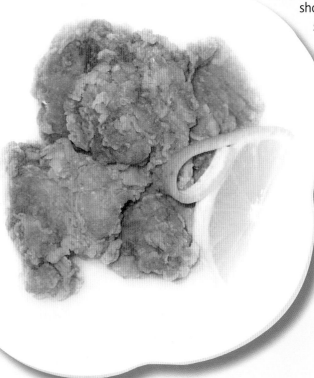

Cut chicken into bite-sized pieces. To make marinade, combine shoyu, ginger, garlic, sugar, salt, pepper, and mirin. Marinate chicken for at least an hour or up to overnight. Drain chicken and lightly dust with cornstarch and flour mixture. Deep-fry in oil until golden and cooked through. Garnish with slice of lemon.

Chicken Katsu
Serves 4

INGREDIENTS

8 boneless skinless chicken thighs
Garlic salt and pepper to taste
1 cup flour
3 eggs
1 tablespoon water
1 teaspoon sugar
3 cups panko (Japanese bread crumbs)
Oil for frying

Pat chicken thighs dry with a paper towel, then season with garlic salt and pepper. Lightly dredge chicken in flour and shake off excess. Beat the 3 eggs with water and sugar to make an egg wash. Dredge floured chicken in egg and finally in panko. Deep-fry in oil until golden and cooked through. Serve with Katsu Sauce (see recipe on page 94).

Fried Chicken Drumettes

Serves 4

2 pounds chicken drumettes
1 egg, beaten
½ cup cornstarch
½ cup flour
2 teaspoons garlic salt
1 teaspoon onion powder
1 teaspoon pepper
1 teaspoon salt
Oil for deep frying

Combine chicken with beaten egg. Then mix together cornstarch, flour, garlic salt, onion powder, pepper, and salt to make a seasoned flour. Dredge chicken drumettes in seasoned flour, shake off excess, and deep-fry until golden and cooked through.

Furikake Chicken Drumettes

Serves 4

INGREDIENTS

6 tablespoons shoyu
2 eggs
1 clove garlic, minced
4 tablespoons flour
6 tablespoons cornstarch
4 tablespoons sugar
2 tablespoons furikake
2 pounds chicken drumettes
1 cup flour
1 cup cornstarch
2 tablespoons + 2 teaspoons furikake
Oil for deep-frying

Combine shoyu, eggs, garlic, 4 tablespoons flour, 6 tablespoons cornstarch, sugar, and 2 tablespoons furikake in a large bowl and mix well. Add chicken, toss well, and marinate overnight. When ready to cook, combine flour, cornstarch, and furikake in a large bowl and mix well. Drain marinade from the chicken, and dredge chicken in flour mixture. Fry in hot oil until golden and cooked through.

Garlic Chicken Fried Rice
Serves 4

10 ounces chicken tenders, cut into ¼- to ½-inch pieces
2 cloves minced garlic
2 tablespoons shoyu
½ teaspoon pepper, divided
2 eggs, beaten
2 tablespoons oil
6 cups day-old cooked rice
1½ tablespoons oyster sauce
½ cup frozen peas and carrots
1 tablespoon chopped chives

Marinate chicken in garlic, shoyu, and ¼ teaspoon pepper for 15 minutes. In the meantime, scramble beaten eggs and reserve. Add oil to a large pan and cook marinated chicken on medium-high heat until cooked through. Add rice, oyster sauce, and pepper. Mix to evenly distribute seasonings. Add peas and carrots and cook until fried rice is heated through. Remove from heat and fold in eggs and chopped chives.

Homemade Chicken Breast Nuggets
Serves 3

INGREDIENTS

1 pound chicken breast tenders, cut in half or thirds (depending on size)
Salt and pepper to season
½ cup flour
2 eggs, beaten
1 cup bread crumbs
Oil for deep-frying

Season a chicken tender with a little salt and pepper. Lightly dredge chicken in the flour, then in beaten egg, and lastly in bread crumbs. Repeat process until all of the chicken is breaded. Deep-fry in hot oil until nuggets are cooked through and golden brown.

Korean Chicken
Serves 4

INGREDIENTS

8 boneless skinless chicken thighs (or 2 pounds chicken drumettes)
2 eggs, beaten
¾ cup flour mixed with ¾ cup cornstarch
Oil for frying

Cut chicken thighs into bite-sized pieces and toss in beaten eggs. Dredge chicken in flour and cornstarch mixture and shake off excess. Deep-fry in oil until golden brown and cooked through. Dip in Korean Dipping Sauce (recipe follows) before serving.

Korean Dipping Sauce

INGREDIENTS

1 cup shoyu
¾ cup sugar
1 tablespoon garlic, minced
1 tablespoon sesame oil
2 tablespoons sliced green onions
2 teaspoons toasted sesame seeds

Heat shoyu, sugar, garlic, and sesame oil until sugar dissolves. Cool, then add green onions and sesame seeds.

Misoyaki Chicken
Serves 4

INGREDIENTS

½ cup white miso
½ cup shoyu
½ cup sugar
½ cup creamy peanut butter
½ cup chicken broth
¼ teaspoon grated ginger
1 teaspoon minced garlic
1½ pounds boneless skinless chicken thighs

Combine miso, shoyu, sugar, peanut butter, chicken broth, ginger, and garlic in a large bowl. Reserve ½ cup of marinade to brush on chicken after cooking. Add chicken thighs to the large bowl and toss in marinade. Marinate overnight and grill or pan-fry until done.

Mochiko Chicken
Serves 4

INGREDIENTS

1½ pounds boneless skinless chicken thighs
4 tablespoons mochiko
4 tablespoons cornstarch
4 tablespoons sugar
5 tablespoons shoyu
2 eggs
1 clove garlic, minced
Oil for frying

Cut chicken into bited-size pieces. Mix mochiko, cornstarch, sugar, shoyu, eggs, and garlic, then marinate chicken overnight. Shake off excess marinade and deep-fry in oil until cooked through and golden brown.

Shoyu Chicken Drumettes
Serves 3

INGREDIENTS

1½ pounds chicken drumettes
1 clove garlic, minced
⅓ cup sugar
⅓ cup shoyu
2 teaspoons mirin
1 teaspoon sesame oil
Sliced green onions and sesame seeds for garnish

In a pot combine chicken, garlic, sugar, shoyu, mirin, and sesame oil. Bring to a boil, then lower heat to medium-low. Simmer for 25 minutes until chicken is tender. Garnish with green onions and sesame seeds.

Teriyaki Chicken
Serves 4

1 cup shoyu
¼ cup peanut butter
¾ cup sugar
3 cloves garlic, crushed
¼-inch thumb-sized slice ginger, crushed
3 stalks green onion, cut into 1-inch pieces
1½ pounds chicken thighs

Combine shoyu, peanut butter, sugar, garlic, and ginger in a sauce pot. Heat until sugar and peanut butter have dissolved. Cool marinade and reserve ¼ of the sauce. Add green onions and chicken thighs to marinade and soak overnight. Grill or broil chicken until cooked through. Baste with reserved sauce after chicken is cooked.

Teriyaki Sauce
Makes 1 quart

INGREDIENTS

2 cups shoyu
2 cups sugar
¼ cup mirin
6 stalks green onion, cut into 1-inch pieces
4 (¼-inch) slices ginger, crushed
4 cloves garlic, crushed

Combine shoyu, sugar, mirin, green onion, ginger, and garlic in a bowl. Mix well until all the sugar dissolves. Store in the refrigerator.

Fried Shrimp
Serves 3

INGREDIENTS

1 pound cleaned large shrimp with tails on
Salt and pepper to season
½ cup flour
2 eggs, beaten
2 cups panko (Japanese bread crumbs)

Dry shrimp on paper towels and lightly season with salt and pepper. Except for the tail, lightly dust shrimp in flour, then in egg wash, then in panko. Repeat the process until all shrimp are done. Deep-fry until golden and cooked through.

Furikake Salmon
Serves 3

6 (3-ounce) steak cuts of salmon
1 cup Teriyaki Sauce (see page 108 or use store-bought), ⅛ cup reserved for after salmon is cooked
Furikake

Marinate salmon in teriyaki sauce overnight and no longer than 8 hours. Drain salmon and sprinkle each cut with ½ teaspoon of furikake. Preheat the oven to 450 degrees and spray an aluminum foil-lined baking tray with nonstick cooking spray. Cook in the oven for about 5 minutes until salmon is almost cooked. Salmon will continue to cook after it is pulled from the oven. Drizzle with reserved Teriyaki Sauce when serving, about 1 teaspoon of sauce per piece.

Garlicky Shrimp
Serves 3

INGREDIENTS

1 tablespoon olive oil
1 tablespoon butter
2 cloves minced garlic
1 pound large shrimp, shelled (except for tail) and deveined
¼ teaspoon salt
⅛ teaspoon pepper
2 teaspoons chopped chives
Lemon slices for garnish

In a sauté pan on medium-high heat, heat olive oil and butter, then sweat garlic. Do not overcook garlic. Add shrimp and season with salt and pepper. Sauté until just cooked, remove from heat, and toss in chives. Serve with lemon slices.

Shrimp Spring Rolls
Serves 6 as a side

½ pound ground pork
¼ pound shrimp, chopped into ¼-inch pieces
¼ teaspoon finely minced garlic
1 tablespoon thinly sliced green onions
⅛ cup chopped reconstituted dried shiitake mushrooms
½ teaspoon sesame oil
½ teaspoon salt
¼ teaspoon pepper
1 egg, beaten and divided
About 24 wonton wrappers

1. Combine pork, shrimp, garlic, green onions, mushrooms, sesame oil, salt, pepper, and half of the egg in a bowl and mix well. Place 1 tablespoon of the mixture at one corner of the wonton wrapper.

2. Roll corner over to make the spring roll and tuck in the corners.

3. Seal the end of the spring roll with a little of the beaten egg. Deep-fry until golden and cooked through.

Shrimp Tempura
Serves 4

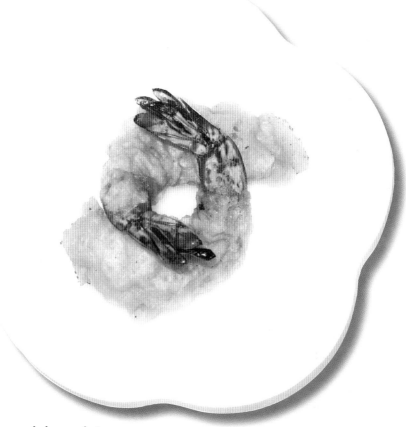

INGREDIENTS

1½ pounds large shrimp
1 egg
1 cup iced water
1 cup flour
Oil for frying

Clean and devein shrimp, leaving only the tails on. Pat shrimp dry on paper towels. Mix egg, iced water, and flour. Keep the bowl with the batter on ice to keep it chilled. Dip shrimp into batter and deep-fry in preheated oil until golden and cooked through.

Stuffed Salmon

Serves 3

INGREDIENTS

6 (3-ounce) cuts of salmon

2 slices bacon, cooked crisp and crumbled (or 3 tablespoons store-bought bacon bits)

3 tablespoons thawed frozen chopped spinach, excess liquid squeezed out

3 ounces imitation crab meat, shredded

1½ tablespoons shredded Parmesan cheese

3 tablespoons mayonnaise

1½ tablespoons panko (Japanese bread crumbs)

Pinch salt and pepper (plus more for seasoning)

¼ cup flour

Oil for frying

Lemon wedges for serving

Cut a slit lengthwise into the side of the salmon, almost all the way through. Mix bacon, spinach, imitation crab, Parmesan, mayonnaise, panko, and pinch of salt and pepper. Divide mixture into 6 equal portions and stuff into the slit of the salmon. Lightly season salmon, dust with flour, and pan-fry with oil on medium-high heat until salmon is almost cooked. Salmon will continue to cook when pulled from the pan.

Chap Chae
Serves 4

NOODLES

INGREDIENTS

4 ounces bean thread
6 dried shiitake mushrooms
1 egg, beaten
3 tablespoons shoyu
2 tablespoons sugar
1 tablespoon sesame oil
2 teaspoons mirin
2 teaspoons toasted sesame seeds
2 teaspoons salt
1 teaspoon pepper
1 tablespoon oil
1 small carrot, julienned
½ medium-sized onion, thinly sliced
2 cloves garlic, minced
¼ cup green onions, sliced

In a pot with boiling water cook bean thread for about 4 to 5 minutes until cooked. Drain and reserve. Soak dried shiitake mushrooms in hot water until reconstituted. Drain mushrooms, thinly slice, and reserve. Spray a small pan with nonstick spray and cook beaten egg on medium-low heat. Do not stir. Flip omelet when it sets, remove from heat, then thinly slice and reserve. Combine shoyu, sugar, sesame oil, mirin, sesame seeds, salt, and pepper in a large bowl. Then in a small pan add oil and sauté carrots, onion, garlic, and shiitake mushrooms for about 2 minutes. Add vegetables and bean thread to the large bowl with the sauce and mix well. Garnish with egg and green onions.

Chicken Long Rice
Serves 4

2 (1.875-ounce) packages long rice
1 tablespoon oil
1 pound chicken thighs or breasts, cut into ¼-inch slices
1 clove garlic, minced
2 (14.5-ounce) cans chicken broth
1 small (thumb-sized) piece ginger, sliced
1 teaspoon Hawaiian salt
¼ teaspoon pepper
1 tablespoon sliced green onions

Cook long rice in boiling water for about 4 to 5 minutes, then drain and set aside. Heat oil in a pan and cook chicken and garlic until cooked through. Stir in chicken broth, ginger, salt, and pepper and long rice. Let simmer for 15 minutes on medium-low heat. Garnish with sliced green onions before serving.

Chicken Yakisoba
Serves 4

1 pound yakisoba noodles (follow directions on package on how to prepare noodles for cooking)

12 ounces boneless skinless chicken thighs or breasts, cut into ¼-inch slices

1 tablespoon shoyu

1 teaspoon mirin

½ teaspoon salt

¼ teaspoon pepper

1 small clove garlic, minced

1½ tablespoons oil

1 small carrot, julienned

1 cup bean sprouts

¼ cup kamaboko, julienned

3 tablespoons oyster sauce

½ teaspoon hondashi (Japanese bonito fish soup base)

¼ teaspoon pepper

3 stalks green onion, cut into 1-inch pieces

Prepare yakisoba for cooking by loosening noodles with your hands or by running them under hot water. In a bowl marinate cut chicken in a mixture of shoyu, mirin, salt, pepper, and garlic for about 10 minutes. In a hot large pan, add oil and chicken; cook until chicken is cooked through. Add carrots, yakisoba, bean sprouts, kamaboko, oyster sauce, hondashi, and pepper. Cook and mix until seasonings are well distributed and noodles are heated through. Toss in green onions and remove from heat.

Citrus Soba Salad
Serves 4 to 6

INGREDIENTS
1 (8-ounce) package soba
1 small carrot, julienned
½ Japanese cucumber, julienned
¼ cup thinly sliced green onions
½ uzumaki (steamed fish cake with a spiral pattern)
Citrus Shoyu Dressing (recipe follows)

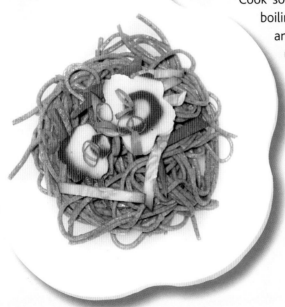

Cook soba for about 5 minutes in boiling water. When done, drain and run under cold water until cool. Drain soba well and place into a bowl. Top noodles with carrots, cucumber, green onions, and fish cake. Pour Citrus Shoyu Dressing (recipe follows) over salad before serving.

Citrus Shoyu Dressing

INGREDIENTS
⅓ cup shoyu
⅓ cup salad oil
⅓ cup sugar
⅓ cup lemon juice (or lime juice if desired)

Combine all ingredients and mix well.

Fried Udon

Serves 3 as a side dish

INGREDIENTS

1 (14-ounce) package udon
1 tablespoon oil
4 ounces char siu, julienned ⅛-inch wide
½ small carrot, julienned ⅛ inch
¼ small onion, sliced into ¼-inch pieces
1½ teaspoons shoyu
¼ teaspoon pepper
1½ teaspoons salt
1½ teaspoons sugar
¼ bag bean sprouts (about 2½ ounces)
2 stalks green onion, cut into 1-inch pieces

Cook udon noodles in boiling water until soft. Drain well. In a large pan on medium-high heat, add oil, char siu, carrot, and onion and cook halfway. Add udon, shoyu, pepper, salt, and sugar and mix well. Add bean sprouts and green onions and cook for another 30 seconds.

Furikake Imitation Crab Noodles
Serves 6 as a side

INGREDIENTS

½ pound thin spaghetti or angel hair pasta
3 fluid ounces oriental dressing
2 tablespoons furikake
½ pound imitation crab meat, shredded
½ large Japanese cucumber, cut in half lengthwise and thinly
   sliced crosswise
Sliced green onions for garnish

Cook pasta until done, cool under cold water, and drain well. Toss noodles with oriental dressing, furikake, imitation crab, and cucumber. Garnish with sliced green onions.

Korean Sesame Soba
Serves 6 as a side

2 bundles soba (about 8-ounce weight uncooked)
1 small carrot, julienned
1 small Japanese cucumber, julienned
¾ cup kamaboko, julienned or cut into shapes
2 stalks green onion, thinly sliced
Sesame Dressing (recipe follows)
Toasted sesame seeds for garnish

Cook soba noodles in boiling water for about 5 minutes. Drain and run under cold water to cool. Drain well and toss with carrots, cucumber, kamaboko, ½ of the green onions, and half of the dressing. Garnish with sesame seeds and the rest of the green onions. Serve with the rest of the dressing on the side.

Sesame Dressing

¼ cup shoyu
¼ cup sesame oil
¼ cup mirin
1 tablespoon sugar
1 small clove garlic, minced
2 stalks thinly sliced green onion
1 teaspoon toasted sesame seeds
¼ teaspoon kochujang (Korean fermented hot pepper and soybean paste)

Combine all ingredients in a jar and shake well to mix. Shake well before using.

Soba

Serves 6

INGREDIENTS

1 (12.7-ounce) package soba
½ cup soba noodle soup base (store-bought) mixed with
1½ cups water
1 cup shredded nori
½ cup green onions, thinly sliced

Cook soba noodles in boiling water for about 5 minutes. Drain and run under cold water to cool. Drain well and serve topped with nori and green onions along with the soba sauce.

Somen

Serves 3 as a side

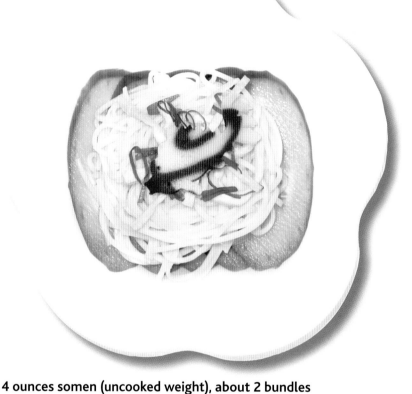

INGREDIENTS

4 ounces somen (uncooked weight), about 2 bundles
1 egg, beaten
½ cup uzumaki (steamed fish cake with a spiral pattern), julienned
½ Japanese cucumber, julienned
2 stalks green onion, thinly sliced
Somen sauce (store-bought)

Cook somen in boiling water until done, about 3 minutes. Drain and run under cold water to cool. Drain somen well. Cook egg like an omelet, cool when done, and thinly slice. Place somen in a bowl and top with uzumaki, cucumber, egg, and green onions. Serve chilled with somen sauce.

Thai Peanut Noodles

Serves 4

INGREDIENTS

8 ounces (uncooked weight) angel hair pasta
1 bunch butter or Mānoa lettuce
1 small carrot, julienned
1 small Japanese cucumber, julienned
1 cup bean sprouts
3 stalks green onion, thinly sliced
4 sprigs Thai basil (optional)
¼ cup toasted chopped peanuts or macadamia nuts
Black sesame seeds for garnish
Thai Peanut Dressing (recipe follows)

Cook angel hair pasta until al dente. Drain and run under cold water to cool. Drain pasta well. To serve, use a few leaves of lettuce, like a bowl, to hold noodles. Top with carrot, cucumber, bean sprouts, green onions, basil, peanuts, and black sesame seeds. Serve with Thai Peanut Dressing.

Thai Peanut Dressing

INGREDIENTS

¼ teaspoon grated ginger
½ teaspoon grated garlic
½ cup shoyu
½ cup peanut butter
½ cup sugar
¼ cup sesame oil
¼ cup oil
¼ cup Japanese rice vinegar

Combine ginger, garlic, shoyu, peanut butter, sugar, sesame oil, oil, and vinegar in a sauce pot and warm to dissolve sugar and peanut butter. Refrigerate and shake well before using.

Vietnamese Vermicelli Noodle Salad

Serves 4 as a side

INGREDIENTS

6 ounces vermicelli (uncooked weight)
1 head butter or Mānoa lettuce
1 small carrot, julienned
1 small Japanese cucumber, julienned
2 stalks green onion, thinly sliced
¼ cup chopped toasted peanuts
4 sprigs mint (optional)
Dressing (recipe follows)

Cook vermicelli noodles and when done, run under cold water to cool. To serve, use a few leaves of the lettuce as a cup to hold the noodles in. Top the noodles with carrot, cucumber, green onions, nuts, mint, and Dressing.

Dressing

INGREDIENTS

½ cup apple cider vinegar
½ cup sugar
1 teaspoon ketchup
¼ cup carrot, julienned

In a sauce pot, heat vinegar, sugar, and ketchup until all of the sugar dissolves. Cool completely and then add carrot.

Bean Sprout Namul
Serves 4 as a side

INGREDIENTS

1 (10-ounce) bag bean sprouts
¾ teaspoon salt
¼ teaspoon pepper
1 teaspoon sesame oil
½ teaspoon toasted sesame seeds
2 tablespoons thinly sliced green onions

Blanch bean sprouts in boiling water for about 10 seconds. Drain hot water and run under cold water to cool. Take small handfuls of bean sprouts and lightly squeeze out excess water. Combine sprouts with salt, pepper, sesame oil, sesame seeds, and green onions. Chill until ready to serve.

Chicken Salad
Makes enough for 4 large sandwiches

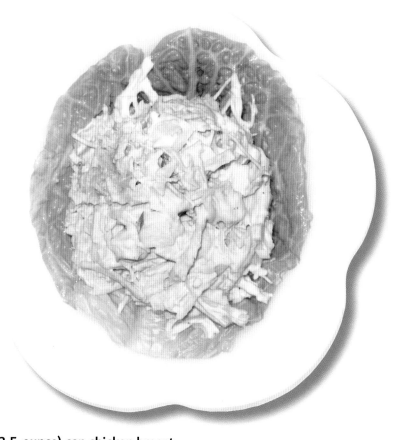

INGREDIENTS

1 (12.5-ounce) can chicken breast
½ cup mayonnaise
¼ cup apples, diced into ¼-inch cubes
2 tablespoons minced celery
2 tablespoons minced onion
Pinch salt and pepper

In a bowl, combine chicken, mayonnaise, apples, celery, onion, salt, and pepper. Serve on bed of lettuce.

Chikuwa Hotdogs

Serves 4 as a side

INGREDIENTS

2 hotdogs
1 chikuwa (tubular-shaped Japanese steamed fish cake)

Either pan-fry or boil hotdog to cook. Set cooked hotdog aside to cool. Cut chikuwa into 2 pieces that are as long as the hotdog. Stuff cooled hotdogs into chikuwa and slice to serve.

Chinese Salad with Crispy Noodles
Serves 4 as a side

½ pound spring greens (or other kinds of lettuce)
1 small cucumber, thinly sliced
1 small carrot, julienned
1 stalk celery, thinly sliced on the bias
2 stalks green onion, thinly sliced
½ cup fried chow mein noodles or fried wonton strips (store-bought)
Cilantro and toasted sesame seeds to garnish (optional)
Hoisin Vinaigrette (recipe follows)

Arrange greens in a bowl and toss with cucumber, carrot, celery, and green onions. Top with fried noodles (or fried wonton); garnish with cilantro and toasted sesame seeds. Serve with Hoisin Vinaigrette.

VARIATION:

🌸 Add cooked shredded chicken, julienned char siu, or Chinese roast pork for a heartier salad.

Hoisin Vinaigrette

½ cup salad oil
¼ cup sesame oil
2 teaspoons Hoisin sauce
¼ cup Japanese rice vinegar
2 tablespoons shoyu
1 teaspoon salt
¼ teaspoon pepper
¼ cup sugar

Combine all ingredients in a jar and shake well to mix. Shake well before serving.

Macaroni Salad

Serves 6 as a side

INGREDIENTS

6 ounces (uncooked weight) elbow macaroni
3 ounces imitation crab, shredded
2 teaspoons grated carrots, squeezed of excess liquid
1 cup mayonnaise
1 teaspoon minced celery
1 teaspoon minced onion
½ teaspoon salt
¼ teaspoon pepper
¼ teaspoon sugar
⅛ teaspoon hondashi (Japanese bonito fish soup base)

Cook macaroni until soft, drain well, and cool completely. In a large bowl combine macaroni with imitation crab, carrots, mayonnaise, celery, onion, salt, pepper, sugar, and hondashi. Mix well and refrigerate for 4 hours. Before serving, mix well and add more mayonnaise if needed.

Potato Macaroni Salad
Serves 6 as a side

INGREDIENTS

2 ounces (uncooked weight) elbow macaroni
1 large russet potato, cleaned and cut into ½-inch cubes
4 ounces imitation crab, shredded
¼ cup frozen peas and carrots, thawed
1 hard-boiled egg, cleaned and cut into ¼-inch pieces
½ cup or more mayonnaise
¼ teaspoon hondashi (Japanese bonito fish soup base)
½ teaspoon salt
½ teaspoon pepper
¼ teaspoon sugar

Cook macaroni and potatoes in separate pots until soft, then drain well and cool completely. Add macaroni and potatoes to a large bowl with imitation crab, peas and carrots, egg, mayonnaise, hondashi, salt, pepper, and sugar. Mix well and refrigerate for at least 4 hours. Before serving, mix well and add more mayonnaise if needed.

Sesame Broccoli

Serves 4 as a side

3 cups broccoli florets
½ teaspoon salt
½ teaspoon shoyu
½ teaspoon sesame oil
½ teaspoon toasted sesame seeds
1 tablespoon thinly sliced green onion

Blanch broccoli florets in boiling water for about 1 minute. Drain hot water and run under cold water to cool. Drain broccoli well and combine with salt, shoyu, sesame oil, sesame seeds, and green onions. Chill until ready to serve.

Shoyu Hotdogs

Serves 4 as a side

INGREDIENTS
....

4 hotdogs, sliced on the bias
¼ cup shoyu
¼ cup sugar

Add hotdogs, shoyu, and sugar to a small pot. Cook on medium until heated through.

Tamago

Serves 4 as a side

INGREDIENTS

4 eggs
1 tablespoon sugar
1 teaspoon mirin
1 tablespoon water
½ teaspoon salt
Nonstick pan spray

Beat together all ingredients. Heat a tamago (egg) pan (or a 6-inch nonstick frypan) over medium-low heat and spray with nonstick pan spray. Pour about ¼ cup of egg mixture into the pan and let cook until almost set; do not stir. From one end of the pan, roll one side of the egg over about 1 inch and continue to roll egg over until the end. Spray pan again and pour in another ¼ cup of egg mixture. Repeat the process until all of the egg mixture is used. Let cool slightly before cutting into slices.

VARIATIONS:

- *To make* CHAR SIU TAMAGO, *add 2 tablespoons minced char siu to egg mixture.*
- *To make* FURIKAKE TAMAGO, *add 1 tablespoon furikake to egg mixture.*
- *To make* FISH CAKE TAMAGO, *add 2 tablespoons minced fish cake to egg mixture.*

Tofu with a Sesame-Shoyu Sauce

Serves 4 to 6 as a side

INGREDIENTS

1 block tofu
½ cup shoyu
2 tablespoons sesame oil
½ teaspoon minced garlic
2 tablespoons thinly sliced green onion
1 teaspoon toasted sesame seeds
1 tablespoon sugar
⅛ cup Japanese rice vinegar
¼ teaspoon pepper

Cut tofu into bite-size dpieces and place on a plate. Combine shoyu, sesame oil, garlic, green onions, sesame seeds, sugar, vinegar, and pepper in a jar and shake well. When serving, shake well and serve sauce on the side or pour over the top.

Tuna Salad

Makes enough for 2 large sandwiches

1 (6-ounce) can tuna
¼ cup mayonnaise
1 tablespoon sweet pickle relish
Pinch onion powder
Pinch salt and pepper

In a bowl combine tuna, mayonnaise, relish, onion powder, salt, and pepper. Serve on bed of lettuce.

Tools

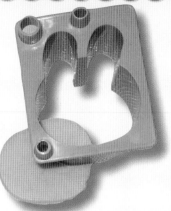
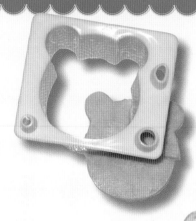

All of the tools with the exception of the Japanese tools, that I used to cut or shape the food, can be purchased locally at specialty kitchen supply stores or at Japanese specialty stores. I obtained the Japanese tools via a very popular Internet auction website. In order to find the tools, go to the website, click on the section "stores" and type in the word "bento." Once you have done so, a listing of several bento stores along with their products will pop up on your computer.

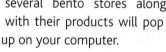

Glossary

CHAR SIU: Chinese barbequed sweet roast pork

CHIKUWA: Tubular-shaped Japanese steamed fish cake

FURIKAKE: Japanese dried rice seasoning

HAN EBI: Japanese colored shrimp flakes used in sushi

HONDASHI: Japanese bonito fish soup base

KAMABOKO: Japanese steamed fish cake

KOCHUJANG: Korean fermented hot pepper and soybean paste

MUSUBI: Japanese rice balls

NAMUL: General term for Korean seasoned vegetables

NORI: Dried sheets of seaweed

SOBA: Japanese buckwheat noodles

SOMEN: Thin white Japanese wheat flour noodles

TAMAGO: Japanese term for eggs

UZUMAKI: Steamed fish cake with a spiral pattern

Bento Index

Hula Girl with Chicken Long Rice and Kālua Pork • 8

Ice Cream with Chicken Adobo • 75

Japanese Girl with Shoyu Chicken Drumettes and Fried Udon • 10

Keiki Sandwich • 55

Ladybug Hamburger • 22

Mandoo Mice • 36
Mermaid with Hotdog Octopus and Fried Shrimp • 66
Mice with Corned Beef Hash and Potato Macaroni Salad • 38
Missy Mouse with Asian Turkey Burgers and Chinese Salad with Crispy
    Noodles • 40
Mouse Sandwich • 54

Octopus with Bacon and Portuguese Sausage Fried Rice • 68
Owl SPAM® Musubi with Fish Cake Tamago • 26
Owl with Pork Gyoza • 24

Pandas with Chicken Karaage • 39
Penguin SPAM® Musubi with Macaroni Salad • 69
Pig Char Siu Fried Rice • 70
Pumpkin Patch with Tamago and Fried Chicken • 71

Rabbit Musubis with Kalbi and Bean Sprout Namul • 42
Roast Pork Mouse Bao • 57

Sheep with Tonkatsu • 43
Snowman with Stuffed Salmon and Fish Cake Tamago • 72
Sun-wich • 58
Surfer Boy with Chap Chae and Barbeque Beef • 12

Teriyaki Meatball Worm with Furikake Imitation Crab Noodles • 73
Tiger with Bacon-and-Corn Chowder • 44

Whale with Shrimp Tempura • 74

Recipe Index

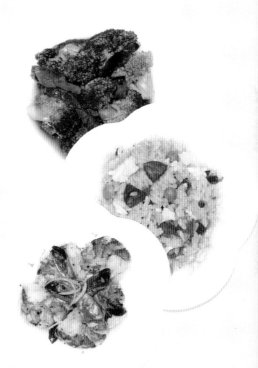

About the Author

Susan was born and raised in Hilo, Hawai'i, and moved to Honolulu, where she continues to reside. She and her husband Mark have two children, Paige, five, and Sean Patric, one.

Following her move to Honolulu, Susan worked in the food industry for many years. Her love for cooking and feeding people eventually led her to a career as a sous-chef at two well-known local restaurants, Palomino Euro-Bistro and Kincaid's, as well as a co-owner of a catering company. In 2002, she gave birth to Paige, whose beautiful smile and loving nature facilitated her decision to become a full-time wife and mother.